Let's Hear It For

Yorkshire Terriers

Written by

Piper Welsh

rourkeeducationalmedia.com

www.rourkeeducationalmedia.com

PHOTO CREDITS: Cover: © khunaspix; page 4: © Ksenia Krylova; page 5,19 © Eric Isselee; page 6: © Eric IsselÃƒÂ©e (Cavalier King Charles Spaniel, Pug), © Stanislav Tolubaev (Pomeranian); page 7: © Nataliya Kuznetsova; page 8: © Eric IsselÃƒÂ©e (Russell Terrier, Cairn Terrier), © Erik Lam (Bull Terrier); page 9: © Kiya; page 11: © Stephen Mcsweeny; page 12: © Pavel Timofeev; page 13: © Bonzami Emmanuelle; page 14: © Lynn M. Stone; page 15: © Carlos Arranz; page 16: © Cynoclub; page 17: © Elizabeth Engle; page 18: © Karina Kononenko; page 20: © Phase4photography; page 21: © Konstantin Pukhov; page 22: © Eric Isselee

Edited by: Precious McKenzie

Cover design by: Renee Brady
Interior design by: Ashley Morgan

Library of Congress PCN Data

Welsh, Piper.
  Let's Hear It For Yorkshire Terriers / Piper Welsh.
    p. cm. -- (Dog Applause)
  Includes index.
  ISBN 978-1-62169-867-8 (hardcover)
  ISBN 978-1-62169-762-6 (softcover)
  ISBN 978-1-62169-968-2 (e-Book)
Library of Congress Control Number: 2013936478

Also Available as:

ROURKE'S e-Books

Rourke Educational Media
Printed in the United States of America,
North Mankato, Minnesota

Rourke
Educational Media
rourkeeducationalmedia.com
customerservice@rourkeeducationalmedia.com • PO Box 643328 Vero Beach, Florida 32964

Table of Contents

Some Yorkie owners like to accentuate their looks with bows or clothes.

Yorkshire Terriers

The Yorkshire Terrier is one of the toy dog **breeds**. Being one of the toy breeds simply means that a dog is lap-sized. But a Yorkie almost looks like a very fancy toy with its dark, button-sized eyes and nose.

Yorkshire Terrier Facts

Weight:	0-7 pounds (0-3 kilograms)
Height:	8-9 inches (21-23 centimeters)
Country of Origin:	England
Life Span:	14-16 years

Perhaps no other breed, for its size, has a coat as long and silky as the Yorkie. The Yorkshire Terrier's coat has helped make it a favorite breed of people who like small, long-haired dogs.

Cavalier King Charles Spaniel

Pug

Pomeranian

There are many different breeds of dogs in the toy group.

The long, soft hair of the Yorkie give it an elegant appearance.

But if a Yorkie looks fancy, it doesn't act that way. These little dogs, like many other terriers, were developed to find, attack, and kill rats. People don't choose Yorkies for their rat-catching ability any longer. But modern Yorkies still have the energy and courage of their **ancestors**.

Russell Terrier

Cairn Terrier

Bull Terrier

Yorkshire Terriers are related to other terrier breeds.

Look at Me!

A Yorkshire Terrier with a full, combed coat looks a bit like it's wearing a robe. Its long fur reaches from its back to the ground, hiding the dog's legs and its tail. Its muzzle hair is combed in a wide, drooping mustache. The forehead ribbon locks up long fur that would otherwise cover the dog's eyes.

Yorkie pups are born black and tan. As they age, they gain the adult colors of tan and shades of gray, usually described as blue.

History of the Yorkshire Terrier

The Yorkshire Terrier's roots are not in fancy grooming and show rings. Instead, people in Yorkshire, England, developed the Yorkie in the 1800s as a **ratter**.

They **crossed** several breeds of terriers, probably

including the Waterside, Clydesdale, and Maltese, among others.

The Waterside Terrier was probably a major ancestor of the Yorkie. A Scottish dog, the Waterside was a small, blue-gray terrier with fairly long hair.

Spending time outdoors gives Yorkies a chance to get rid of their boundless energy.

The Yorkie's soft, silky coat makes it one of the most handsome of all the toy breeds.

No one knows if the English were trying to develop an especially beautiful terrier. But that is what they got. By the late 1800s, Yorkshire Terriers were being shown by wealthy owners in England and America.

The Yorkie's size makes it a perfect lap-dog or sometimes even a purse-dog!

Many of the early Yorkies weighed between 12 and 14 pounds (5 and 6 kilograms). Yorkie owners decided they preferred smaller dogs, so they began choosing only smaller Yorkies to be parent dogs. Today's Yorkshire Terriers are not supposed to weigh more than 7 pounds (3 kilograms).

Some Yorkie owners clip or groom them with a shorter cut while others like their natural, long hair.

Don't be fooled by a Yorkshire Terrier's small size. They are brave, loyal dogs that enjoy action and adventure.

Yorkies can be trained for agility and are quite smart and athletic.

The American Kennel Club (AKC) accepted the Yorkshire Terrier onto its list of official breeds in 1885. In the United States, the Yorkshire Terrier was the sixth most popular breed for 2012.

The Right Dog for You?

Yorkies are friendly and playful dogs. They love games, and they like to fetch. Anyone who owns a Yorkie should be willing to play games with the dog.

A tennis ball is among one of the Yorkies most valued possessions.

The size of the Yorkie makes it convenient to take just about anywhere.

Yorkshire Terriers are so independent that they aren't always easy to teach. However, they can be taught **obedience** and even **agility** by a patient owner.

Yorkies on-leash like a short hike, but as a rule they are not outdoor dogs. They are small enough to get good exercise just by romping in the home.

Many Yorkie owners show their dogs. Yorkshire Terriers with ribbons on their foreheads and finely combed body fur are ready for the show ring.

Did you know...

The dog that Sharpay Evens carries in the movie High School Musical 2 is a Yorkie.

Yorkies with long fur need combing or brushing almost every day. People who don't show their Yorkshire Terriers often trim their fur, especially during the warm months.

Despite their small size, Yorkshire Terriers make good watchdogs. Like other terriers, Yorkies are quick to bark at strangers.

Yorkies are alert and very protective of their owners.

Although small in size, the Yorkie seems to think he is bigger than he really his.

Sometimes Yorkies act like they have no idea how small they are. They can be **aggressive** toward other dogs.

And just because Yorkshire Terriers are small doesn't mean they should be left alone with small children.

Doggie Advice

Puppies are cute and cuddly, but only after serious thought should anybody buy one. Puppies grow up.

And remember that a dog will require more than love and patience. It will need healthy food, exercise, grooming, a warm, safe place in which to live, and medical care.

A dog can be your best friend, but you need to be its best friend, too.

Choosing the right breed requires some homework. For more information about buying and owning a dog, contact the American Kennel Club at *www.akc.org/index.cfm* or the Canadian Kennel Club at *www.ckc.ca.*

Glossary

agility (uh-JIL-u-tee): the ability to perform certain athletic tasks, such as leaping through a hoop

aggressive (eh-GRES-iv): wanting to attack or attacking

ancestors (AN-SES-turz): animals that at some past time were part of the modern animal's family

breeds (BREEDZ): particular kinds of domestic animals within a larger, closely related group, such as the Yorkshire Terrier breed within the dog group

crossed (KROSSD): to have been mated with an animal of a different breed

obedience (o-BEED-ee-unts): the willingness to follow someone's direction or command; a pre-set training program for dogs

ratter (RAT-ur): a dog developed and used mostly for finding and killing rats

Index

Websites to Visit

www.akc.org/breeds

www.dogbreedinfo.com/yorkshireterrier.htm

www.yorkshireterrier-training.com

Show What You Know

1. What is the life span of a Yorkshire Terrier?

2. What kind of dog breed is the Yorkshire Terrier?

3. What color are Yorkie pups when they are born?